Have You Ever Judged Someone Based On Your First Impression?

Never, Ever,
Judge a Book,
By Its Cover!

By: Kelly Emrick, MBA, Ph.D.

Introduction

In this book, I explore the importance of being observant and the dangers of making snap first impressions. Our fast-paced and ever-changing world often tempts us to make quick judgments about people and situations without truly understanding them. However, this approach can lead to missed opportunities, misunderstandings, and even harm.

Through personal observations, anecdotes, and scientific research, I will delve into the benefits of being observant and showing empathy can help you build stronger relationships that lead to better decision-making. I will also examine how our preconceptions and biases can cloud our judgment and lead us to form inaccurate impressions.

By learning to be more observant and resist the urge to make snap judgments, you can improve your relationships, expand your understanding of the world, and lead more fulfilling personal and professional lives. Whether you are a business professional, a student, or looking to improve your relationships and personal growth, this book will provide the tools and insights you need to become more observant and open-minded.

Because we are social beings, humans continuously engage with and assess others around us. We accomplish this, among other things, by passing judgment on other people. Why do we do this? Several psychological theories make an effort to explain why we judge others.

According to one view, we judge people to comprehend and foresee their conduct. We make assumptions about future behavior based on prior experiences and observations. As a result, we can manage social situations more successfully and efficiently by judging others.

According to a different hypothesis, we judge others to create social hierarchies. We can ascertain our standing and place within a group by assessing and contrasting ourselves against others. We might also find possible partners and enemies by evaluating how we stack up against others.

Furthermore, making assumptions about other people might be used for selfish gain. We may increase our self-esteem and feel good about ourselves by making false narratives about others. Negatively assessing others might give us a sense of superiority and strength.

It is essential to remember that passing judgment on others may also have unfavorable effects. For instance, it may result in bias and discrimination and negatively affect mental health. Therefore, it is crucial to be conscious of our prejudices and make an effort to interact with others in an empathic and understanding manner.

Humans have a natural tendency to make judgments about others quickly and easily. Making judgments about others is a fundamental aspect of human nature that has evolved as a means of survival. For example, our ancestors needed to quickly assess potential threats and allies to survive in a hostile environment. However, this tendency to judge others rapidly in today's modern world can have negative consequences.

One of the main reasons that humans are quick to make judgments about others is because of cognitive biases. These biases are inherent in the way that our brains process information. For example, the halo effect is a cognitive bias that causes us to form an overall positive or negative impression of a person based on a single characteristic. This means that if we see someone well-dressed and articulate, we may assume that they are also intelligent and competent, even if we have no evidence to support this assumption.

Another reason that humans are quick to make judgments about others is because of social stereotypes. We tend to group people based on their race, gender, sexual orientation, religion, and other characteristics. We then assume that all group members share the same characteristics, even if this is not the case. This can lead to discrimination and prejudice.

The tendency to quickly make judgments about others can also be influenced by the context in which we meet someone. For example, if we are in a formal setting, such as a job interview, we may be more likely to make judgments based on a person's appearance rather than their qualifications.

However, it is not all negative, as our ability to quickly make judgments about others can also have positive consequences. For example, it can help us quickly identify trustworthy and reliable people. It can also help us to allow strong social bonds with others.

In summary, the tendency to quickly make judgments about others is a primary aspect of human nature. While it can have negative consequences, such as discrimination and prejudice, it can also have positive consequences, such as the ability to identify trustworthy people quickly. Therefore, it is essential to be aware of our natural tendency to make judgments about others and to actively strive to be non-judgmental to build stronger, more inclusive communities.

Chapter One
First Impressions

First impressions are powerful. They often shape how we perceive and interact with others, and they can be hard to change once they are formed. Nevertheless, why do we rely so heavily on first impressions? Several psychological theories explain why we judge others based on first impressions.

According to one view, the necessity for effective information processing causes people to establish initial impressions fast. Humans are restricted in their ability to digest information, so when we meet someone new, we must decide if they are friends or enemies. We swiftly assess others by using cognitive shortcuts like physical appearance.

Another hypothesis is that initial impressions are influenced by prior knowledge and expectations. For example, we frequently label and stereotype individuals based on their physical characteristics, ethnicity, gender, or other bodily characteristics. These assumptions and preconceptions influence our perceptions of and interactions with others. Our preconceived prejudices can also impact first impressions. For instance, we could tend to have favorable first impressions of people who are similar to us and opposing first impressions of those who are different from us.

For various reasons, poor judgment can result from snap judgments about other people. One explanation is that first judgments are frequently made hastily and without all the information required. For example, when we meet someone new, we frequently judge their outward appearance to form opinions about them. These conclusions, however, could not be a true reflection of the person's actual traits or mannerisms.

It may also lead to preconceptions and prejudices, so making snap judgments about others can lead to impaired judgment. These preconceptions and stereotypes can affect how we view and relate to others, resulting in bias and discrimination.

Our biases and prejudices can also impact how we see other people. For example, positive first impressions of people similar to us may be easier to develop than negative first impressions of those different from us. This may result in a lack of variety and inclusion in our social interactions and the loss of meaningful connections. Furthermore, passing judgment on someone based just on appearances can be harmful to the individual passing judgment. People with a wrong first impression may be excluded from chances or positions or face discrimination and prejudice. Their mental and emotional well-being may suffer as a result.

Chapter Two
Why People Are Bad At Judging Others:
The Psychology of First Impressions

The ability to judge others accurately based on a first impression is a complex process influenced by various psychological factors. However, research has shown that people are often bad at judging others based on a first impression due to several cognitive biases and heuristics that can lead to inaccurate and unfair judgments.

One critical psychological factor contributing to poor first-impression judgments is confirmation bias. Confirmation bias refers to the tendency for people to seek out, interpret, and remember information in a way that confirms their preconceptions and beliefs. This bias can lead people to pay more attention to information that confirms their initial impressions of others while disregarding information that contradicts it.

Another important psychological factor that contributes to poor first-impression judgments is the halo effect. The halo effect refers to people's tendency to judge others based on a single characteristic or trait. For example, if someone is attractive, we may assume they are also intelligent and kind. This bias can lead people to make inaccurate and unfair judgments about others based on superficial characteristics.

The fundamental attribution error is another psychological factor contributing to poor first impression judgments. The fundamental attribution error refers to the tendency for people to overestimate the role of dispositional factors (e.g., personality or character) in explaining other people's behavior while underestimating the role of situational factors. This bias can lead people to make inaccurate and unfair judgments about others based on their behavior in a specific situation without considering the context in which it occurred.

Furthermore, the availability heuristic is another psychological factor contributing to poor first impression judgments. The availability heuristic refers to the tendency for people to rely on information that is readily available to them rather than seeking out more accurate and complete information. This bias can lead people to make judgments about others based on limited or superficial information rather than taking the time to gather more complete and accurate information.

In summary, understanding the psychological factors that contribute to poor first impression judgments can help us to be more aware of the biases and heuristics that can lead to inaccurate and unfair judgments. By being aware of these factors, we can overcome them and make more accurate and fair judgments about others based on a first impression. This can lead to better relationships, a more harmonious society, and a better understanding of others.

Chapter Three
Biases of Judging Others

Judging others based on first impressions can be influenced by various biases. These biases can distort our perceptions and lead to inaccurate judgments about others.

One bias that can influence first impressions is the halo effect. The halo effect is the tendency to form a positive overall impression of someone based on one positive characteristic. For example, if someone is attractive, we may assume they are also intelligent, kind, and successful.

Halo Effect Bias

The halo effect is a cognitive bias that refers to the tendency to form a positive overall impression of someone based on one positive characteristic. This bias can significantly impact how we perceive and judge others, particularly regarding first impressions.

One of the main ways in which the halo effect can manifest is through physical appearance. For example, attractive people are often seen as more intelligent, kind, and successful. This bias can be seen in various settings, such as hiring, dating, and social interactions. For example, a study found that physically attractive individuals were more likely to be hired, promoted, and receive higher salaries than their less attractive counterparts, even when their qualifications were the same.

The halo effect can also be seen in how we perceive experts or authority figures. People seen as experts or authority figures in a particular field are often assumed to be more competent and trustworthy in other areas.

Another way the halo effect can manifest is through how we perceive celebrities. People who are famous or well-known are often assumed to be more talented, successful, and even morally superior to others. This can lead to a lack of critical evaluation of their abilities and perpetuate stereotypes and myths.

The halo effect can also lead to a self-fulfilling prophecy. For example, when we assume someone is competent, we may be more likely to give them opportunities and resources, which can lead to their success. On the other hand, if we assume someone is less competent, we may be more likely to limit their opportunities, which can limit their success.

It is essential to be aware of the halo effect and to strive to overcome it. This can be done by actively seeking and considering information that contradicts our initial impressions and being aware of the potential for bias in our perceptions and judgments. Additionally, consciously evaluating people based on their qualifications and abilities rather than physical appearance, status, or fame can counteract the halo effect.

To summarize, the halo effect is a cognitive bias that refers to the tendency to form a positive overall impression of someone based on one positive characteristic. This bias can significantly impact how we perceive and judge others, particularly regarding first impressions. Furthermore, it can manifest in various ways, such as through physical appearance, expertise, fame, or other manifestation. Therefore, to overcome the halo effect, it is vital to be aware of it, actively seek out information that contradicts our initial impressions, and evaluate people based on their qualifications and abilities rather than physical appearance, status, or fame.

Confirmation Bias

Another bias that can influence first impressions is confirmation bias. Confirmation bias is the tendency to seek out and interpret information in a way that confirms our pre-existing beliefs and attitudes. For example, if we have a negative attitude towards someone, we may be more likely to notice and remember negative information about them while ignoring positive information.

Confirmation bias is a cognitive bias that refers to the tendency to seek out and interpret information in a way that confirms our pre-existing beliefs and attitudes. This bias can significantly impact how we perceive and judge others, particularly regarding first impressions.

Confirmation bias can manifest in a variety of ways. One way it can manifest is through selective attention. People tend to pay more attention to information confirming their pre-existing beliefs and attitudes and less to information that contradicts them. This can lead to a self-reinforcing cycle where people become more and more entrenched in their beliefs and less open to alternative perspectives.

Another way confirmation bias can manifest through the way we interpret information. People tend to interpret ambiguous or neutral information in a way that confirms their pre-existing beliefs and attitudes. This can lead to a distorted perception of reality and prevent people from seeing the true complexity of a situation.

Confirmation bias can also lead to a self-fulfilling prophecy. When people expect a particular outcome, they may act in ways that make that outcome more likely to occur, such as interpreting ambiguous information to confirm their expectations.

Confirmation bias can be particularly detrimental in decision-making. People tend to rely on their pre-existing beliefs and attitudes when faced with complex decisions and may overlook vital information that contradicts those beliefs. This can lead to poor decisions and negative consequences for both individuals and society as a whole.

To overcome confirmation bias, it is crucial to be aware of it and seek and actively consider alternative perspectives. This can be done by actively seeking out and considering evaluating what contradicts our initial beliefs and attitudes, being open to alternative perspectives, and being aware of the potential for bias in our perceptions and judgments. Additionally, practicing critical thinking and questioning our assumptions can help counteract confirmation bias.

To summarize, confirmation bias is a cognitive bias that refers to the tendency to seek out and interpret information in a way that confirms our pre-existing beliefs and attitudes. This bias can manifest in various ways, such as through selective attention, interpretation of information, and self-fulfilling prophecy. Confirmation bias can be particularly detrimental in decision-making. To overcome it, it is vital to be aware of it, actively seek out and consider alternative perspectives, critically practice thinking, and question our assumptions.

Fundamental Attribution Error Bias

A third bias is the fundamental attribution error. This is the tendency to attribute other people's behavior to internal characteristics, such as personality or disposition, while attributing our behavior to external factors, such as the situation. This can lead to the assumption that people's behavior reflects their character when it may affect the environment or situation.

The fundamental attribution error (FAE) is a cognitive bias that refers to the tendency to over-attribute the behavior of others to their internal characteristics, such as personality or abilities, rather than to situational factors. This bias can significantly impact how we perceive and judge others, particularly regarding first impressions.

The FAE can manifest in a variety of ways. One way it can manifest is through dispositional inference, where people tend to infer the personality traits or abilities of others based on their behavior. For example, suppose someone observes another person behaving rudely. In that case, they may infer that the person is rude by nature rather than considering the situational factors that may have led to the behavior.

Another way the FAE can manifest is through the actor-observer bias, where people tend to attribute their behavior to situational factors but attribute the behavior of others to their internal characteristics. For example, suppose someone performs poorly on a test. In that case, they may attribute the failure to situational factors such as a stern test while attributing the success of others to their abilities.

The FAE can also lead to a self-fulfilling prophecy. When people expect a particular outcome, they may act in ways that make that outcome more likely to occur, such as interpreting ambiguous information to confirm their expectations.

The FAE can be particularly detrimental to social interactions. When people attribute the behavior of others to their internal characteristics, they may overlook the situational factors that led to the behavior, leading to misunderstandings and negative judgments of others.

To overcome the FAE, it is vital to be aware of it and to consider situational factors when making judgments about others actively. This can be done by actively seeking out information about the context in which the behavior occurred, considering alternative explanations for the behavior, and being aware of the potential for bias in our perceptions and judgments. Additionally, practicing perspective-taking, in which we try to understand the point of view of the other person, can also help to counteract the FAE.

To summarize, the fundamental attribution error FAE is a cognitive bias that refers to the tendency to over-attribute the behavior of others to their internal characteristics, such as personality or abilities, rather than to situational factors. This bias can manifest in various ways, such as through dispositional inference, actor-observer bias, and self-fulfilling prophecy. The FAE can be particularly detrimental to social interactions. To overcome it, it is crucial to be aware of it, actively consider situational factors when making judgments about others, practice perspective-taking, and question our assumptions.

Stereotype Bias

The stereotype bias is fourth. This is the inclination to make assumptions about people based on their physical appearance, race, gender, and so on. This might lead to the perception that people adhere to their group's expectations rather than being viewed as individuals. Stereotypes are widely held ideas or assumptions about a group of individuals based on incomplete or superficial knowledge. Stereotypes can be based on ethnicity, gender, age, sexual orientation, and other factors. Stereotyping can cause biases in our perceptions and interactions with others.

The stereotype threat is one of the most well-known biases connected with stereotypes. Individuals belonging to a negatively stereotyped group may suffer anxiety or dread of confirming the stereotype, resulting in lower performance or self-esteem. For example, if a woman is taking a math test and is aware of the stereotype that women are bad at arithmetic, she may become anxious and do poorly on the test.

Confirmation bias is another prejudice connected with stereotypes. This refers to our propensity to seek and interpret information in ways that reinforce our pre-existing opinions or prejudices. For example, assume someone believes that all Asians are skilled at arithmetic. In that instance, people may selectively recall or interpret facts to reinforce their beliefs, even if the evidence says otherwise.

Another prejudice connected with stereotypes is the halo effect. The halo effect is the propensity to believe that people who are good at one thing are equally good at another. So, for example, if someone is strong in arithmetic, we may presume they are also clever, trustworthy, and so on.

Another prejudice linked with stereotypes is the false-consensus effect. The false-consensus effect is the propensity to overestimate how much others share our opinions and attitudes.

We must be conscious of these biases and actively evaluate our narratives and assumptions to overcome them. This may be accomplished by searching out and examining evidence that contradicts our assumptions, challenging our stereotypes' origins, and remaining open to new information and views. Furthermore, regularly connecting with people from other backgrounds may expose us to fresh viewpoints and knowledge and aid in mitigating the impact of preconceptions.

Finally, stereotypes are commonly held opinions or assumptions about a particular group based on little or superficial knowledge. Stereotype threat, confirmation bias, halo effect, and false-consensus effect are all examples of biases caused by stereotypes. Therefore, we must be conscious of these biases and actively evaluate our stories and assumptions to overcome them. Furthermore, regularly connecting with people from other backgrounds may expose us to fresh viewpoints and knowledge and aid in mitigating the impact of preconceptions.

Blind Spot Biases

Blind spot bias is a cognitive bias in which people are oblivious to their own biases and how they affect their perceptions and behaviors. This prejudice is especially harmful since it is frequently unconscious, making it challenging to recognize and change.

The Dunning-Kruger effect is a well-known example of blind spot bias. This refers to the phenomenon in which people with limited aptitude in a specific domain overestimate their talents. This is because students must acquire the information and skills necessary to appropriately appraise their talents, which causes them to overestimate their performance. This is seen in academics, work performance, and driving abilities.

The bias blind spot is another form of blind spot bias. This is the phenomenon in which people are aware of their prejudices yet feel less vulnerable to them than others. This is because they feel they are more reasonable and objective than others; therefore, they overestimate their capacity to resist prejudices.

Individuals' perceptions and interactions with others might also exhibit blind spot bias. For example, assume that someone prejudices a specific group of individuals. In such a scenario, they may need to be made aware of how this stereotype influences their perceptions and interactions with members of that group. This can result in prejudice, decision-making bias, and a lack of empathy.

To avoid blind spot bias, we must be conscious of the possibility of prejudice and actively seek out and examine material that contradicts our views and preconceptions. This may be accomplished through soliciting input, being open to new ideas and opinions, and actively connecting with individuals from varied backgrounds. Mindfulness methods, such as meditation, can also promote self-awareness and lessen unconscious biases' impact.

To conclude, blind spot bias is a cognitive bias in which people are oblivious to their own biases and how they affect their perceptions and behaviors. This prejudice is especially harmful since it is frequently unconscious, making it challenging to recognize and change. The Dunning-Kruger effect, bias blind spot, and how people perceive and interact with others are all examples of blind spot bias. Therefore, it is critical to be aware of the possibility of bias and to actively seek out and examine material that contradicts our views and assumptions to overcome blind spot bias. Mindfulness methods, such as meditation, can also assist in promoting self-awareness and lessen unconscious biases' impact biases can lead to inaccurate perceptions and judgments of others and negatively affect the person being judged and society as a whole. Therefore, it is essential to be aware of these biases and to strive to overcome them to form more accurate perceptions of others and to promote greater inclusivity and positive social interactions.

Judging others based on first impressions can be influenced by various biases. These biases, such as the halo effect, confirmation bias, fundamental attribution error, stereotype bias, and bias blind spot, can lead to inaccurate perceptions and judgments of others. Therefore, it is essential to be aware of these biases and to strive to overcome them to form more accurate perceptions of others and to promote greater inclusivity and positive social interactions.

Chapter Four

Improve Your First Impression Skills

You may enhance your talents and learn not to offend others based on your initial perceptions by putting crucial approaches into practice. However, it is crucial to remember that this method takes time and effort. Nonetheless, becoming more aware of your prejudices and assumptions might help you learn to interact with people more positively and successfully.

Rapid judgments about other individuals can lead to poor judgment since those snap evaluations do not adequately represent those people's fundamental features or actions. To enhance your talents and avoid making quick judgments about other people, you must go through a process that requires self-awareness and the willingness to change. By practicing mindfulness, challenging your assumptions, educating yourself, seeking out other viewpoints, being open to change, and exercising empathy, you may become more conscious of your biases and prejudices and engage with others more positively and productively.

It takes self-awareness and a commitment to change to improve your abilities and stop making snap judgments about people. Listed below are some helpful tactics:

1. By practicing mindfulness, you may be present at the moment and notice your thoughts and feelings without passing judgment. In addition, mindfulness training can help you become more aware of your biases and prejudices and learn how to cope with them constructively.

2. Take a step back when meeting someone new and challenge your previous thoughts about them.

Consider if your view of them is based on fact or preconceived notions. Consider them as individuals rather than stereotypes.

3. Get educated: Discover the many backgrounds, cultures, and experiences. This allows you to question your beliefs and prejudices and better comprehend and respect the diversity of individuals worldwide.

4. Seek out diverse perspectives by surrounding oneself with people of various experiences, nationalities, and cultures. This may prompt you to reconsider your assumptions and prejudices, allowing you to see the world from various perspectives.

5. Be flexible: Recognize that your beliefs and attitudes may shift, and be open to new insights and experiences. Be willing to question your assumptions and beliefs and make the necessary changes.

It might be challenging to determine what to believe when assessing others. People frequently generate ideas based on experiences, prejudices, and inadequate knowledge. However, there are various approaches to judging the acts and character of others that are more fair and truthful.

First, gathering as much information as possible about the person in question is essential. This includes not only their actions but also their motivations, beliefs, and context. Additionally, it is necessary to consider multiple perspectives, including those that may disagree with your point of view.

Next, it is important to question one's own biases and assumptions. Everyone has prejudices and preconceptions that can cloud their judgment. By being aware of these biases and trying to overcome them, one can make a more objective assessment of the person in question.

Another crucial step is applying critical thinking and logical reasoning when evaluating available information. This includes being skeptical of information not supported by evidence and is open to the possibility that one's initial assumptions may be incorrect.

Finally, it is essential to remember that people are complex and multi-faceted and that no single action or characteristic can fully define a person. Therefore, rather than making snap judgments based on limited information, it is vital to consider a person's actions and character in the context of their lives and experiences.

To summarize, assessing others may be difficult. Still, one may make a more fair and accurate judgment of people by acquiring information from numerous sources, evaluating one's prejudices, employing critical thinking, and noting the complexity of others.

Chapter Five
Keeping An Open Mind

Keeping an open mind when meeting someone for the first time is essential for creating healthy and meaningful connections. An open mind allows for understanding and interaction with others rather than dismissing them based on preconceived notions or assumptions. Here are some ideas to help you retain an open mind while meeting new individuals.

1. Get rid of preconceived notions: It is easy to form opinions about someone based on their appearance, background, or other superficial characteristics. However, these expectations might make it challenging to connect with someone. Instead, discard preconceived notions and approach the person with a blank slate.

2. Be inquisitive: Being curious about someone's life, experiences, and perspectives is an excellent strategy for maintaining an open mind. Ask questions, actively listen, and show genuine interest in learning about the person you are meeting.

3. Be open to other points of view: It is normal to disagree and hold opposing viewpoints, but it is critical to address these differences with an open mind. Recognize that everyone has different experiences and viewpoints, and be willing to learn from them.

4. Empathy: Putting oneself in another person's shoes is valuable for understanding and connecting with people. Consider where the individual comes from and what led to their thoughts or actions.

5. Be mindful: Being wholly engaged with the person you are meeting at the current time will help you stay

focused and avoid becoming distracted by your thoughts or preconceptions.

6. Be open to change: People might surprise us at times. Remember that people may change, develop, and progress. Recognize that individuals may change and may not be the same person you initially met.

By following these recommendations, you may have an open mind when meeting someone for the first time and build stronger, more enduring relationships. Remember that everyone is different and that understanding and connecting with people necessitates an open mind. To make fair and accurate judgments while analyzing others, it is necessary to match facts and source information kept in memory. This approach can be complex because individuals usually draw judgments based on incomplete information, preconceptions, and prior experiences.

However, there are a few methods for matching facts while judging others. First, getting as much information as possible on the person in issue is critical. This covers their acts, intentions, beliefs, and surroundings. Furthermore, evaluating diverse opinions, including those that may conflict with yours, is critical.

1. Organize Information: Once you have gathered information, it is essential to organize it to make it easy to access and match it with other facts and information. This might include creating a chart or list of the information and its source or creating a mental map of the information in your head.

2. Verify Information: Verify the information you have collected by cross-referencing it with other sources. Be skeptical of information not supported by

evidence, and be open to the possibility that one's initial assumptions may be incorrect.

3. Use Reasoning: When evaluating the information, use critical thinking and logical reasoning to connect the dots and to understand the person's behavior and character.

4. Remember that people are complex: People are complex and multi-faceted, and no single action or characteristic can fully define a person. Remembering this complexity will help you to avoid making snap judgments based on limited information.

In summary, matching facts and source information stored in memory when judging others is crucial in making fair and accurate assessments. By gathering information, organizing it, verifying it, reasoning, and remembering that people are complex, one can effectively match facts and source information stored in memory when judging others.

Chapter Six
Your Misconceptions and Stereotyping

Misconceptions and stereotypes can have a powerful influence on how we judge others. These misconceptions can be stubborn and difficult to correct, but it is essential to understand and correct them to make fair and accurate assessments of individuals. Here are several strategies for understanding and correcting stubborn misconceptions when judging others.

1. Recognize your biases: It is essential to be aware of them, as they can influence how you perceive and judge others. Reflect on preconceptions or stereotypes and how they may affect your perceptions of others.

2. Challenge assumptions: Challenge assumptions and stereotypes by questioning their validity and seeking alternative perspectives. Ask yourself if your beliefs are based on evidence or if they are based on preconceptions or stereotypes. Seek out diverse perspectives: Seek out diverse perspectives and actively listen to individuals who hold different beliefs or come from different backgrounds. This can help you understand a situation's complexity and correct any misconceptions.

3. Be open to new information: Be available to new information and be willing to adjust your perceptions and beliefs in light of new evidence. Remember that our understanding of the world is constantly evolving, and being mindful of these changes essential.

4. Take responsibility for your misconceptions: If you realize you have misconceptions about someone,

take responsibility for them. Apologize if necessary, and commit to correcting them in the future.

Following these strategies makes it possible to understand and correct stubborn misconceptions when judging others. Remember that misconceptions and stereotypes can have a powerful influence on how we perceive and judge others. Still, by being aware of our biases and seeking out diverse perspectives, we can make fair and accurate assessments of individuals.

People are often quick to form opinions and judge others, even before they have all the information. Unfortunately, these premature judgments can lead to mental misconceptions, which can result in a wide range of negative consequences.

There are several reasons why people make mental misconceptions about others, even before they have all the information. One of the main reasons is that people are naturally wired to form quick opinions and judgments. This is a survival mechanism that dates back to our earliest ancestors, who needed to assess potential threats and dangers in their environment quickly.

Another reason for mental misconceptions is that people often rely on stereotypes and past experiences to form opinions about others. For example, suppose someone has had a bad experience with a particular group of people. In that case, they may be more likely to form negative opinions about that group in the future, even if they do not have all the facts. People can make many different types of mental misconceptions about others. Some of the most common misconceptions include the following:

1. Racism and discrimination: People may make negative assumptions about others based on their race, ethnicity, or national origin.

2. Ageism: People may make negative assumptions about others based on their age, such as assuming that older people are incapable of adapting to new technology or that younger people are irresponsible.

3. Sexism: People may make negative assumptions about others based on gender, such as assuming that women are not as competent as men in specific jobs.

4. Stereotypes: People may make negative assumptions about others based on cultural, ethnic, or racial stereotypes. For example, someone may assume that all Muslims are terrorists or that all African Americans are criminals.

The consequences of mental misconceptions can be severe and far-reaching. Some of the most common consequences include the following:

1. Prejudice and discrimination: Mental misconceptions can lead to prejudice and discrimination, which can cause individuals to

experience harm and discrimination based on their race, ethnicity, or national origin.

2. Stigma: Mental misconceptions can also lead to stigma, which can cause individuals to experience adverse social and psychological effects based on their age, gender, or sexual orientation.

3. Isolation and exclusion: Mental misconceptions can lead to isolation and exclusion, which can cause individuals to feel disconnected from their communities and excluded from meaningful social and professional opportunities.

To summarize, individuals frequently create snap judgments and depend on stereotypes and prior experiences to form conclusions about others. Mental misunderstandings can lead to prejudice and discrimination, stigma, isolation, and exclusion. To reduce the detrimental impacts of mental errors, educating individuals about the hazards of making snap judgments and encouraging them to seek knowledge and engage in open and honest communication with others is critical.

Chapter Seven

Falsehoods Travel Faster Than Truths

The psychology of how falsehoods travel further and faster than the truth has been a research topic for decades. Studies have shown that false information can spread rapidly and reach more people than accurate information. This phenomenon has been attributed to several psychological factors, including the tendency to seek and remember information that confirms our beliefs and the emotional appeal of false information.

1. Confirmation bias: People tend to seek and remember information that confirms their beliefs while disregarding information that contradicts them. This can spread false information, as people are likelier to share and believe information that confirms their pre-existing beliefs.

2. Emotional appeal: False information can often be more emotionally appealing than factual information. For example, a false rumor about a celebrity's death may be more likely to be shared than a factual article about their health. This is because people are more likely to be motivated to share information that evokes strong emotions, such as fear or anger, rather than neutral information.

3. Social influence: False information can spread quickly through social networks, as people are more likely to believe and share information endorsed by others. The more people believe and share a piece of information, the more likely it is to be perceived as trustworthy.

4. The speed of the internet: The internet and social media platforms have made it easier for false information to spread quickly. False information can travel worldwide in seconds, reaching millions of people before it can be fact-checked or debunked.

5. The role of misinformation in the political sphere: Misinformation is also used as a political tool to manipulate public opinion and to sow discord. Misinformation can create confusion and mistrust and sway opinions, especially on social media platforms.

Falsehoods travel further and faster than the truth due to several psychological factors, including confirmation bias, emotional appeal, social influence, internet speed, and misinformation's role in the political sphere. Therefore, it is essential for individuals to be critical and discerning consumers of information and to fact-check information before sharing it. Additionally, media literacy and digital literacy education may help to reduce the spread of misinformation.

Making accurate judgments and first impressions about others is essential to human interaction, but it can also be challenging. Our biases, assumptions, and stereotypes often influence our judgments and first impressions. Therefore, it is important to use techniques that can help us to be more realistic when making judgments and first impressions about others.

1. Recognize and admit your prejudices: Recognizing and admitting your own biases is an essential first step toward forming more accurate assessments and initial impressions. Consider your preconceived notions or prejudices and how they may influence your impressions of others.

2. Active listening focuses entirely on the person speaking without interrupting or forming assumptions. As a result, you are more likely to catch up on tiny hints and nonverbal communication when you actively listen, which can help you make more accurate judgments and initial impressions.

3. Seek out numerous viewpoints: It is critical to recognize that individuals come from various backgrounds, experiences, and opinions. Therefore, seek out numerous opinions and carefully listen to those with different beliefs or experiences. This can help you appreciate the complexities of a situation

and make more realistic judgments and initial impressions.

4. Give people the benefit of the doubt: It is easy to jump to conclusions, but it is essential to give people the benefit of the doubt. Assume the best of people, and avoid making negative judgments or first impressions based on limited information.

5. Be open to change: Remember that people can change and that our understanding of others constantly evolves. Therefore, be open to new information and be willing to adjust your perceptions and judgments in light of new evidence.

The abovementioned techniques can improve your ability to make realistic judgments and first impressions about others. In addition, recognizing and acknowledging your own biases, practicing active listening, seeking out multiple perspectives, giving people the benefit of the doubt, and being open to change are all critical steps in making more accurate and fair assessments of individuals.

Chapter Eight

How Effective Leaders Bypass First Impressions

Influential leadership recognizes that the initial interview with someone is a pivotal chance to learn about their abilities, experience, and possible fit for a job inside the firm. Therefore, one primary method prominent leaders thrive in this process is to conduct interviews nonjudgmentally.

Bein benign is essential in your judgments of others. This means going into the interview with an open mind and a desire to listen to and learn from the applicant. It entails putting aside preconceived preconceptions or biases and concentrating on candidates' qualities, abilities, and experience as they apply to the position.

Effective leaders understand that candidates' first impression may not accurately represent their abilities. Therefore, they avoid jumping to conclusions based on superficial factors such as appearance, accents, speech patterns, or other extraneous factors.

By being non-judgmental, influential leaders create a more positive and relaxed environment for the candidate, which allows them to be more open and honest about their qualifications and experience. This can lead to a more accurate assessment of the candidate's fit for the role and a more successful hiring decision in the long run.

Another benefit of being non-judgmental during an interview is that it helps to establish trust and mutual respect between the interviewer and the candidate. As a result, the candidate is more likely to see the interviewer as fair, unbiased, and respectful, which can improve their overall impression of the organization and their willingness to accept a job offer if one is extended.

Influential leaders are non-judgmental when interviewing someone for the first time because it allows them to understand better the candidate's qualifications and fit for the role. In addition, it helps to establish trust and mutual respect between the interviewer and the candidate. By approaching interviews in this way, influential leaders are better equipped to make sound hiring decisions that benefit both the organization and the candidate.

Successful leaders are often known for making accurate and effective decisions about the people they work with. Successful leaders can balance quick decisions with the need for thorough evaluation and analysis when making first-impression decisions about others.

Successful leaders make accurate first-impression decisions by being aware of their biases and actively working to mitigate them. This includes awareness of common biases such as confirmation bias, where individuals look for information that confirms their pre-existing beliefs, and the halo effect, where individuals judge someone based on one positive characteristic. Successful leaders also make an effort to consider multiple perspectives and gather as much information as possible before making a decision.

Another critical factor in accurate first-impression decisions is the ability to read people. Successful leaders have social intelligence and can quickly read and interpret people's body language and nonverbal cues. In addition, they can quickly identify critical characteristics, such as confidence, honesty, and trustworthiness, which can help them form a more accurate impression of a person.

In addition to being aware of their own biases and reading people, successful leaders also make accurate first-impression decisions by being willing to admit when they are wrong and to change their opinion as new information becomes available. They can separate what they know from what they think they know and are open to further information that may change their perception of a person. This allows them to make decisions that are not only accurate but also adaptable to changing circumstances.

In summary, successful leaders can make accurate first-impression decisions by being aware of their own biases, gathering as much information as possible, reading people, and being willing to admit when they are wrong. By following these fundamental principles, leaders can make fair and effective decisions about the people they work with and build strong and successful teams.

Chapter Nine
Methods For Measuring Judgments

The ability to assess others is frequently defined as an acquired feature. This capacity, considered a personality attribute, is sufficiently universal to classify "excellent" and "bad" judges. Contradictions across research may be attributable to the low reliability of the measures employed and the influence of the type of judgment required, attributes appraised, and participants involved. Appropriate judgmental norms appear to be the foundations of this capacity.

Judgmental norms refer to individuals' expectations and standards when evaluating and making decisions about others. A critical aspect of judgmental norms is the similarity between the judge and the subject, which can significantly influence judgments. It is well established that individuals tend to have more favorable judgments of people who are similar to themselves, known as the similarity-attraction effect. This can occur on various levels, including demographic characteristics (e.g., race, gender, age), personality traits, or even attitudes and beliefs. For example, a job interviewer is likelier to favorably evaluate a candidate who shares similar interests, values, or educational background than one who does not.

Using similarity as a basis for judgments can have positive and negative consequences. Similarity can foster understanding and empathy, leading to more accurate and fair evaluations. However, on the other hand, it can lead to a lack of diversity in decision-making and perpetuate bias and discrimination.

To promote fairness and objectivity in decision-making, it is essential to be aware of and actively counteract the influence of similarity on judgment. This can include using multiple sources of information when evaluating individuals, seeking diverse perspectives, and being mindful of one's biases and assumptions.

Another approach is to use demographic diversity in the decision-making team or group. Research has shown that having a diverse group of decision-makers can help to reduce the effects of similarity-attraction bias and lead to more fair and accurate evaluations.

The similarity between the judge and the subject can significantly influence judgmental norms. Therefore, it is essential to be aware of the potential for bias and actively counteract it to promote fairness and objectivity in decision-making. By having a diverse group of decision-makers and using multiple sources of information, organizations can reduce the effects of similarity-attraction bias and lead to better decision-making.

General and Social Intelligence

The ability to judge others through general and social intelligence is perhaps the most difficult to accomplish, due in part to a learned understanding of a person's non-analytic judgment or intuition.

Intuition, also known as a gut feeling or sixth sense, is the ability to understand something without needing conscious reasoning. As a result, it is a powerful tool that can be used to make quick and accurate judgments about people and situations. However, while intuition can be a valuable asset, it is essential to consider various factors when making judgments about others.

One crucial factor to consider is the context of the situation. The same behavior may be interpreted differently depending on the context in which it occurs. For example, an ordinarily punctual person may be viewed as flaky if they are late for a meeting, but their tardiness may be excused if they have a valid reason, such as a traffic accident.

Another factor to consider is the person's past behavior. People tend to act consistently over time, so their past behavior can provide valuable information about how they will behave in the future. However, it is essential to remember that people can change and that past behavior is not always indicative of future behavior.

It is also crucial to consider one's biases and prejudices when making judgments about others. Our preconceptions and biases can cloud our judgment and lead us to form inaccurate impressions. To minimize the influence of biases, it is essential to consider multiple perspectives and to be open to the possibility that our initial impression may be wrong.

Lastly, gathering as much information as possible before judgment is essential. Intuition can be a valuable mental tool but must be relied upon sparingly. Instead, it should be used in conjunction with other forms of information, such as observation and analysis, to form a complete understanding of the person or situation.

In summary, intuition can be a powerful tool for judgments about others. Still, it should be used with other factors such as context, past behavior, personal biases, and gathering information. We can make more accurate and fair judgments about people and situations by considering these factors.

Be very careful not to become overly consumed by your gut feelings. In today's fast-paced and ever-changing world, it is easy to fall into the trap of relying too heavily on our gut feelings when judging others. However, while intuition, or gut feeling, can be a valuable tool, it is essential to remember that it should not be relied upon exclusively. Overly judging someone based on gut feelings can lead to missed opportunities, misunderstandings, and even harm.

One major problem with relying too heavily on intuition is that our biases and prejudices can influence it. Our preconceptions and biases can cloud our judgment and lead us to form inaccurate impressions of others. For example, suppose we have a preconceived notion that people who dress a certain way are less intelligent. In that case, we may be more likely to form a negative impression of someone who fits that stereotype, even if they are knowledgeable.

Another issue with overly judging someone based on our gut feeling is that it can lead to missed opportunities. For example, when we form a negative impression of someone based on our intuition, we may not take the time to get to know them and may miss out on valuable relationships or partnerships.

In addition, overly judging someone based on our gut feeling can also harm our relationships with others. When we form negative impressions of others, we may treat them poorly or dismiss their ideas and contributions, leading to tension and conflict in our relationships.

To avoid these problems, it is essential to remember that intuition should be relied upon sparingly. Instead, it should be used in conjunction with other forms of information, such as observation and analysis, to form a complete understanding of the person or situation. We can make more accurate and fair judgments about people and situations by considering multiple perspectives and gathering as much information as possible.

In conclusion, while intuition can be a valuable tool, it is crucial not to judge someone based on our gut feeling. Instead, by considering multiple perspectives, gathering information, and being aware of our biases and prejudices, we can make more accurate and fair judgments about people and situations and ultimately build better relationships.

Judgmental Motivation

Be cautious of your motivations or biases when making judgments of others. Personal motivation biases can significantly affect how we judge others, and these biases can stem from various personal motivations. Understanding these motivations can help us become more aware of our biases and take steps to overcome them.

One personal motivation that can lead to biases is the need for social acceptance. People often conform to the opinions and attitudes of those around them to fit in and be accepted. This can lead to biases in judgment as individuals may adopt the prejudices of their social group without considering them critically.

Another motivation that can lead to biases is the need for cognitive consistency. People are naturally inclined to seek consistency in their beliefs and attitudes, and when new information is presented that contradicts their existing beliefs, they may reject it to maintain consistency. Again, this can lead to biases in judgment as individuals may ignore or discount information that contradicts their preconceptions.

A third motivation that can lead to biases is self-esteem. People may hold on to positive self-perceptions of themselves by selectively interpreting information to reinforce their positive self-image. This can lead to biases in judgment as individuals may view other people or groups in a more favorable light if they are seen as similar to themselves and in a more negative light if they are seen as dissimilar.

Lastly, past experiences can also lead to biases in judgment. People may develop biases towards certain groups or situations because of past experiences, whether positive or negative. This can lead to biases in judgment as individuals may generalize their past experiences to all people or situations of the same group or type, even if they are not applicable.

In conclusion, personal biases in judging others can stem from various personal motivations, such as the need for social acceptance, cognitive consistency, self-esteem, and past experiences. By understanding these motivations, we can become more aware of our biases and take steps to overcome them. This can lead to more accurate and fair judgments about people and situations and ultimately build better relationships.

Past Experiences on Judgment

Past experiences can profoundly impact our judgment of others and our world perception. Our experiences shape our beliefs, attitudes, and behaviors and influence how we see and interact with others. However, when our past experiences are negative or traumatic, they can also lead to harmful and skewed judgments of others, causing division, hostility, and conflict.

Past experiences can shape our beliefs, attitudes, and behaviors in many ways, significantly impacting our judgment of others. For example, suppose we have had negative experiences with people from a particular cultural background. In that case, we may be more likely to view people from that background negatively and make assumptions about them based on our experience. Likewise, in that case, for certain behaviors, we may be more likely to view people who exhibit those behaviors in a negative light and make negative judgments about them.

To reduce the negative influence of past events on judgment, it is critical to have a more compassionate and understanding attitude toward people and participate in techniques that aid in healing and transforming past experiences. Some strategies that can help with this include:

1. Mindfulness focuses on the present moment and pays attention to our thoughts, feelings, and experiences without judgment. By practicing mindfulness, we can develop greater self-awareness and gain a deeper understanding of our biases and preconceptions, reducing the negative impact of past experiences on our judgment of others.

2. Cognitive-behavioral therapy (CBT) is a type of psychotherapy that assists people in identifying and challenging harmful ideas and actions. Individuals who engage with a therapist can get a better knowledge of their prior experiences and build new, more positive ways of thinking and behaving that reduce the negative influence of their past experiences on their judgment of others.

3. Empathy training: The ability to comprehend and share the feelings of another is referred to as empathy. We may decrease the negative influence of prior events on our judgment of others by exercising empathy and learning to comprehend the viewpoints and experiences of others

Past events can shape our views, attitudes, and behaviors in ways that might lead to damaging and biased

assessments of others. Therefore, it is critical to develop a more compassionate and understanding approach to people, participating in techniques such as mindfulness, cognitive-behavioral therapy, and empathy training to reduce the negative influence of prior experiences on judgment. We may foster a more positive and inclusive society by doing so, as well as lessen the negative influence of our prior experiences on our judgment of others.

Chapter Ten
Perils of Bad Judgement

Making accurate and fair judgments about people is critical for developing and sustaining effective personal and professional relationships. Conversely, the effects can be severe and long-lasting when we form an incorrect initial impression of a person or group of individuals.

One of the most apparent consequences of creating a wrong first impression is the loss of possibilities. We may not try to get to know someone if we have a negative image of them, and we may miss out on potential connections or collaborations. This might result in lost business or missed cooperation chances in a professional situation. In a personal context, it might result in losing friendships or love relationships.

Also, making the wrong first impression can lead to tension and conflict in relationships. When we form negative beliefs about others, about may treat them poorly or dismiss their ideas and contributions. This can lead to hurt feelings, resentment, and even hostility. This can lead to difficulty working together, lack of trust, and reduced productivity in a professional setting.

Making the wrong first impression can also perpetuate stereotypes and discrimination. When we form negative impressions of particular groups of people, we may perpetuate harmful stereotypes and contribute to discrimination. This can harm those who are discriminated against and society as a whole.

Another disadvantage of generating a poor first impression is that it might result in self-fulfilling prophecies. When we have an unfavorable opinion of someone, we may treat them in a way that validates that view, even if it is incorrect. This might create a vicious cycle in which our first impression leads to adverse treatment, reinforcing our first view.

Finally, having the wrong initial impression of a person or group of people can have severe and long-term implications. It can result in missed opportunities, relational friction and conflict, perpetuating prejudices and discrimination, and self-fulfilling prophesies. To build a more accurate and fair view of others, we must be cognizant of our biases and prejudices and obtain knowledge from diverse perspectives.

Making accurate and fair judgments about people is critical for developing and sustaining effective personal and professional relationships. However, overcoming our own biases and preconceptions is not always straightforward. Here are some tips to help you make more accurate and fair assessments of others:

1. Collect information from many sources. It is critical to gather information from diverse sources and views to build a more accurate and fair opinion of someone. This includes asking questions, listening to others, and considering opposing viewpoints. Furthermore, when acquiring information, we must be aware of our biases and preconceptions and deliberately seek opinions that differ from ours.

2. Exercise mindfulness. Being mindful is being aware of our thoughts, feelings, and environment. For example, we may become more conscious of our biases and prejudices by being mindful and taking action to overcome them. Mindfulness practice can also make us more receptive to new ideas and views.

3. Do not rush to judgment. When creating an opinion of someone, it is critical not to leap to conclusions based on inadequate information. Instead, take the time to obtain further information and examine alternative viewpoints. It is also critical not to make conclusions about people based on preconceptions or previous experiences.

4. Consider your previous decisions. Take some time to analyze your previous judgments regarding people and if they were truthful and fair. Reflecting on

previous judgments might assist us in identifying patterns in our thoughts and behavior that may result in biases and prejudices.

5. Accept responsibility for your decisions. Recognize that your actions have real-world repercussions and that you are responsible for them. Accept responsibility for your choices and be open to revising them if new knowledge becomes available.

6. Seek feedback and opinions from others. Seek feedback and viewpoints on your decisions from others. Inquire whether or not they agree with your evaluation and why. This will give you a different perspective on the issue and allow you to make a more accurate and fair assessment.

To recap, developing our ability to make accurate and fair judgments about others is a continuous process that needs self-awareness, attention, and a willingness to evaluate other views. Nevertheless, we may overcome our biases and prejudices and establish more accurate and fair views of people by employing these tactics. This can lead to more harmonious relationships and a more peaceful society.

Chapter Eleven
History Repeats Itself

Throughout history, making wrong first impression assumptions has caused significant changes in events. These assumptions can be based on race, gender, religion, sexual orientation, socioeconomic status, and many other factors. When individuals or groups of people are judged incorrectly, it can lead to various negative consequences that can change the course of history.

While significant progress has been achieved in the last decade regarding class stereotyping assumptions, society still has room to improve. One notable example is how racial beliefs have influenced history. Influential people have historically marginalized and oppressed people of color. This is due, in part, to the perception that people of color are lower and less capable than white people. These preconceptions have resulted in prejudice, segregation, and violence against people of color, with far-reaching consequences throughout history.

Another example is gender assumptions. Women have been marginalized and oppressed by those in authority throughout history. Assumptions that women are weaker, less clever, and less capable than males have resulted in discrimination, segregation, and violence against women, all of which have significantly influenced the course of history.

Religion-related assumptions have also influenced the path of history. Individuals and organizations have been persecuted, discriminated against, and oppressed throughout history because of their religious views. This is partly due to preconceptions that adherents of a particular religion are inferior, harmful, or a threat to society. These preconceptions have resulted in bloodshed, prejudice, and even genocide, with far-reaching consequences throughout history.

Additionally, assumptions about socioeconomic status have also played a role in shaping the course of history. Throughout history, individuals and groups have been marginalized and oppressed due to their socioeconomic status. Assumptions that people from lower socioeconomic backgrounds are less capable, less intelligent, or less worthy have led to discrimination and violence, which has profoundly impacted the course of history.

To summarize, having incorrect first impression judgments has significantly influenced history. These assumptions might be based on criteria such as color, gender, religion, social background, etc. When individuals or groups of people are wrongfully assessed, it can have a wide range of adverse effects that can alter the course of history. As a result, to establish a more just and equal society, we must acknowledge and confront these prejudices and preconceptions.

Chapter Twelve
Educate Yourself

How can one educate themselves on assessing people properly and successfully without prejudice or self-interest? Education is crucial to learning how to properly and fairly assess people without prejudice or self-interest. However, it is essential to remember that it is a constant process and that unlearning prejudices is just as important as learning new ways of thinking. Here are some ways to learn how to assess others successfully and adequately without prejudice, bias, or self-interest:

1. Learn about many cultures, groups, and points of view. Understanding the experiences and views of people and groups that are different from ourselves is critical for establishing an accurate and fair understanding of others. Learning about diverse cultures, communities, and social groupings, as well as comprehending the historical backdrop that has formed their experiences, may be part of this.

2. Recognize and question your prejudices. We all have unconscious biases that impact how we see and judge others. Recognizing and overcoming these biases is critical for gaining proper and accurate knowledge of people. This might involve becoming aware of various forms of prejudices, such as implicit biases, and taking action to mitigate them.

3. Seek out other points of view. It is critical to seek out other points of view in order to understand people more correctly and honestly. This might entail actively listening to and engaging with people and

groups that have different experiences and viewpoints than us.

4. Empathy should be practiced. The ability to comprehend and share the sentiments of others is referred to as empathy. We may obtain a better knowledge of people and make more accurate and fair judgments about them if we practice empathy.

5. Reflect on your past judgments. Reflecting on past decisions can help us to identify patterns in our thinking and behavior that may lead to biases and prejudices. Reflecting on past decisions can also allow us to learn from our mistakes and make more accurate and fair judgments in the future.

6. Seek feedback and perspectives from others. Seek input and perspectives from others on your judgments. Ask them if they agree or disagree with your assessment and why. This will give you another perspective on the situation and help you to form a more accurate and fair judgment.

To summarize, learning how to assess people successfully and adequately without prejudice or self-interest is a continual process that needs self-awareness, attention, and a willingness to accept other views. Using these tactics, you can overcome your biases and prejudices and establish more accurate and fair views of others. This can lead to more harmonious relationships and a more peaceful society.

Chapter Thirteen
Hindsight Judgement

Hindsight judgment, also known as the "hindsight bias," is a cognitive phenomenon in which individuals believe an event or outcome is more predictable or evident than before it occurred. This bias can have significant implications in various fields, including legal proceedings, risk management, and decision-making.

Hindsight bias in court processes can lead to unjust judgments of persons or organizations engaged in an occurrence. A jury, for example, may find a defendant guilty of negligence if they failed to anticipate an unavoidable consequence, even though it was not reasonably foreseeable at the time. In such instances, the criminal may face punishment for something they could not have expected or avoided.

Hindsight bias in risk management can lead to a false sense of security and a lack of preparation for possible future dangers. For example, a business may assume that a particular risk was simple to foresee and manage when, in fact, it was not. As a result, individuals may fail to take the required safeguards to avoid future threats.

Hindsight bias in decision-making may lead to bad judgments by individuals and organizations. For example, an individual may think that a specific option was the best at the time, but in retrospect, a different decision might have been preferable. This might result in a lack of confidence in one's decision-making abilities and a tendency to second-guess oneself.

Individuals and organizations must be aware of the phenomena and actively endeavor to avoid it to lessen its impacts. Techniques such as scenario planning, decision-making under uncertainty, and post-mortem analysis can be used. Furthermore, the possible influence of hindsight bias in legal procedures, risk management, and decision-making processes must be considered. Hindsight bias may also play a role in how we assess others.

First impressions are frequently regarded as one of the most important variables influencing how we see and assess others. However, when it comes to hindsight bias, the propensity to assume that an event or conclusion was more foreseeable or obvious before it occurred, our perception and assessment of others may not be correct.

Individuals may be unfairly judged based on initial impressions due to hindsight bias. For example, a person may be disregarded as unqualified for a job or unfit for a relationship based on how they appear, dress, or speak during the initial meeting, while possessing the required abilities, credentials, or traits to thrive in the role or relationship.

Furthermore, hindsight bias can lead to a distorted perception of persons based on first impressions. For example, a person may assume they have accurately judged another person's character based on their initial look or actions. Even so, they may have only seen a fraction of who the individual genuinely is. Misunderstandings and poor communication can result in both professional and personal relationships.

To lessen the consequences of hindsight bias in making judgments about individuals based on initial impressions, it is critical to be aware of the phenomena and actively tries to prevent it. Examples of this are taking the time to get to know someone beyond their initial look or behavior, asking open-ended questions, attentively listening to their replies, and considering several views before reaching a judgment. Additionally, it is essential to be open to changing one's perception and assessment of a person as more information is learned about them.

Finally, hindsight bias is a cognitive phenomenon that can seriously affect legal procedures, risk management, and decision-making. To make fair, accurate, and productive decisions, individuals and organizations must be aware of this bias and take action to limit its impacts. The inclination to assess individuals based on their initial impressions can result in hindsight bias, which can substantially impact professional and personal relationships. To make fair, accurate, and successful judgments and to create stronger connections with others around us, we must be conscious of this bias and take action to lessen its impact.

Chapter Fourteen
Arm Chair Quarterbacking

Being an "armchair quarterback" refers to the tendency to judge or criticize a situation or decision without having all the relevant information or being directly involved. This term is often used in sports, but it can also apply to other areas of life, including how we make first-impression judgments of others.

When judging people based on first impressions, it is easy to fall into the trap of being an armchair quarterback. We may form opinions about others based on limited information or from a distance without considering the context or the other person's perspective. This can lead to unfair or inaccurate judgments and a lack of understanding of the person we are judging.

For example, in a professional setting, an armchair quarterback might form an opinion about a colleague based on one meeting or a brief interaction without considering the colleague's work history, skills, or experience. Similarly, in a social setting, an armchair quarterback might form an opinion about a person based on their appearance or behavior without considering the person's background or experiences that may have shaped their behavior or appearance.

To avoid the pitfalls of being an armchair quarterback regarding first impression judgments, it is crucial to approach each person with an open mind and actively seek out additional information. This can include taking the time to get to know a person beyond their initial appearance or behavior, asking open-ended questions, listening actively to their responses, and considering multiple perspectives before making a judgment.

Additionally, one must be willing to change one's opinion as more information is learned about the person.

Being an armchair quarterback when judging people based on first impressions can lead to unfair or inaccurate judgments and a lack of understanding of the person we are judging. Therefore, it is essential to be aware of this tendency and actively seek additional information and perspectives before judgment. By doing so, we can make fair and accurate judgments and build better relationships with the people around us.

Chapter Fifteen
Trusting Your Judgements

It is important to question one's first impressions of others because first impressions are often based on superficial and incomplete information. They can be influenced by a person's appearance, behavior, or a single interaction and may not accurately reflect their true character or abilities. By questioning one's first impressions, individuals can avoid making unfair or inaccurate judgments and gain a deeper understanding of the people with whom they interact.

One fundamental way to question one's first impressions is by actively seeking additional information about a person. This can include talking to the person directly, observing their behavior in different situations, and gathering feedback from others. By gathering more information, individuals can gain a complete picture of the person and better understand their strengths, weaknesses, and motivations.

Another essential step in questioning one's first impressions is to be aware of one's own biases and to work to mitigate them actively. This includes awareness of common biases such as confirmation bias, where individuals look for information that confirms their pre-existing beliefs, and the halo effect, where individuals judge someone based on one positive characteristic. By being aware of these biases, individuals can avoid making judgments based on incomplete or skewed information.

In addition to seeking out additional information and being aware of biases, it is also essential to consider multiple perspectives when assessing others. This means looking at a person from different angles and considering different viewpoints. This can help individuals gain a complete understanding of the person they are interacting with and avoid making judgments based on a narrow or limited perspective.

In summary, one must question one's first impressions of others to make accurate assessments. This can be achieved by actively seeking out additional information and being aware that one is biased, considering multiple perspectives. By following these principles, individuals can make fair and accurate judgments about the people they interact with and build more substantial and productive relationships.

Chapter Sixteen
Societal and Cultural Influences

Society and culture play a significant role in shaping our attitudes and beliefs about others. A wide range of cultural and societal factors, including the media, our family and friends, and our personal experiences, influence our perceptions and judgments of others. Further, societal norms, values, and beliefs influence our perceptions and judgments of others. For example, our attitudes toward race, gender, and sexuality are heavily influenced by the norms and values prevalent in our society.

The media often shape our perceptions of others. The media can profoundly impact our attitudes and beliefs about others, particularly regarding portrayals of marginalized groups. For example, if the media consistently portrays a particular group of people as dangerous or criminal, this can influence our perceptions and judgments of that group.

Culture also has a significant impact on our perceptions and judgments of others. Our cultural background can shape our attitudes and beliefs about different races, ethnicities, and nationalities. For example, someone from a culture that values conformity may be more likely to judge others who are seen as "different" or "nonconformist."

Moreover, cultural values and beliefs can shape our perceptions of gender and sexuality. For example, if someone comes from a culture that values traditional gender roles, they may be more likely to judge others who do not conform to these roles.

The effects of societal and cultural influences on our perceptions of others may be severe and far-reaching. The following are some of the most prevalent consequences:

1. Prejudice and discrimination: Prejudice and discrimination can be caused by societal and cultural forces, causing individuals to face damage and discrimination based on their race, ethnicity, or national origin.

2. Stigma: Stigma may be caused by societal and cultural pressures, which can cause individuals to feel negative social and psychological impacts based on their age, gender, or sexual orientation.

3. Isolation and exclusion: Societal and cultural forces can cause individuals to feel alienated from their communities and excluded from significant social and professional possibilities.

To recap, societal and cultural forces profoundly alter our attitudes and ideas about others. Various cultural and societal influences affect our perceptions and judgments of others, including the media, our family and friends, and our personal experiences. These judgments can have severe and far-reaching repercussions, such as bias and discrimination, stigma, isolation, and exclusion. To offset the negative impacts of societal and cultural influences on our judgments, educating individuals about the hazards of these influences and encouraging them to seek out other opinions and engage in open and honest discourse with others is critical.

The Influence of Social Media

Social media has become integral to our daily lives, affecting how we communicate, receive information, and interact. How social media is used can profoundly impact our judgments of others, particularly our perceptions of their character, behavior, and worth.

Social media significantly affects our perceptions of others, particularly regarding our assessments of their character and conduct. Social media influences our perceptions through the information we receive about others through our newsfeeds and other sources. The information we receive about others on social media can be biased, inaccurate, or even false, leading us to form incorrect or skewed judgments of them.

Social media can also influence our perceptions of others through the way they present themselves online. People may present themselves in a particular way on social media, either to present a positive image of themselves or to hide aspects of their personality or behavior that they do not want others to see. This can lead us to form incorrect or skewed perceptions of them.

The consequences of social media-influenced judgments can be severe and far-reaching, affecting both the individuals who are being judged and the people who are making the judgments. Some of the most common consequences include the following:

1. Cyberbullying: Social media-influenced judgments can lead to cyberbullying, which can cause individuals to experience harm and distress due to

negative comments, messages, and other forms of online harassment.

2. Stigma: Social media-influenced judgments can also lead to stigma, which can cause individuals to experience adverse social and psychological effects based on their age, gender, or sexual orientation.

3. Isolation and exclusion: Social media-influenced judgments can lead to isolation and exclusion, which can cause individuals to feel disconnected from their communities and excluded from meaningful social and professional opportunities.

Social media significantly impacts our judgments of others, particularly regarding our perceptions of their character and behavior. The consequences of these judgments can be severe and far-reaching, including cyberbullying, stigma, isolation, and exclusion. To mitigate the adverse effects of social media on our judgments of others, it is essential to educate people about the dangers of these influences and encourage them to engage in open and honest dialogue with others. It is also necessary to be mindful of the information we receive about others through social media and to critically evaluate the information we receive before forming judgments of others.

How we judge others is a complex and multi-faceted process influenced by various factors, including our experiences, beliefs, and values. However, self-reflection and empathy play a crucial role in shaping our judgments of others and can help us to form more accurate and fair assessments of the people around us.

Self-Reflection on How We Judge Other

Self-reflection is examining our thoughts, feelings, and behaviors to understand ourselves and our motivations better. When it comes to our judgments of others, self-reflection can help us to identify our own biases, preconceptions, and blind spots and to challenge these assumptions to form more accurate and fair assessments of others.

An essential component in the judgment of others is how we are empathetic toward others. Empathy is the ability to understand and share the feelings of others. When it comes to the decisions of others, empathy can help us to put ourselves in their shoes and to understand their perspectives and experiences. This, in turn, can help us to form more accurate and fair assessments of others and to avoid making judgments based solely on our own experiences and biases.

To improve our judgments of others, we must reflect and practice empathy in our interactions. Some of the strategies that can help us to do this include:

1. Practicing self-awareness: Self-awareness is the key to self-reflection, and it involves paying attention to our thoughts, feelings, and behaviors to gain a deeper understanding of ourselves and our motivations.

2. Challenging our assumptions: To challenge our assumptions, be open to new information and perspectives, and consider alternative explanations for the behavior of others.

3. Practicing empathy involves putting ourselves in the shoes of others and trying to understand their perspectives and experiences. This can be done through active listening, asking questions, and seeking to understand the experiences of others.

To recap, self-reflection and empathy are essential in influencing our judgments of others and can assist us in developing more accurate and fair assessments of others around us. As a result, we must self-reflect, challenge our preconceptions, and develop empathy to better our connections with others. Doing so may create a more nuanced and compassionate knowledge of people and avoid forming judgments based only on our prejudices and preconceptions.

Conclusion

The Consequences of Judging Others: Negative Effects on Individuals and Society

Judging others is a typical human behavior that can have significant consequences for the individuals being judged and society as a whole. While it is natural to form opinions about others based on their behavior, appearance, and other factors, negative judgments can lead to shame, guilt, and self-doubt in those who are judged. Additionally, negative judgments can create division, foster hostility, and undermine social cohesion, adversely affecting society.

Judging others can have a profound impact on the mental and emotional well-being of those who are judged. For example, negative judgments can lead to shame, guilt, and self-doubt, causing individuals to question their worth and experience low self-esteem. This, in turn, can lead to a range of negative consequences, including depression, anxiety, and a decreased ability to form meaningful relationships with others.

Judging others can also have adverse effects on society as a whole. For example, negative judgments can create division, foster hostility, and undermine social cohesion, leading to a breakdown in trust and communication between individuals and groups. This, in turn, can lead to conflicts, misunderstandings, and social unrest, further exacerbating the harmful effects of judging others.

To improve the adverse effects of judging others, it is vital to adopt a more compassionate and understanding approach to others. Some of the strategies that can help to do this include:

1. Cultivating empathy: Empathy is the ability to understand and share the feelings of others. By practicing empathy, we can gain a deeper understanding of the perspectives and experiences of others and avoid making negative judgments based solely on our own experiences and biases.

2. Challenging negative assumptions: Negative assumptions about others can lead to negative judgments and contribute to the harmful effects of judging others. By challenging these assumptions and seeking to understand the perspectives and experiences of others, we can avoid making negative judgments and reduce the adverse effects of judging others.

3. Engaging in self-reflection: Self-reflection examines our thoughts, feelings, and behaviors to understand ourselves and our motivations better. By self-reflection, we can identify and challenge our biases and preconceptions and avoid negative judgments about others.

Final Thought:
The Most Important Among All

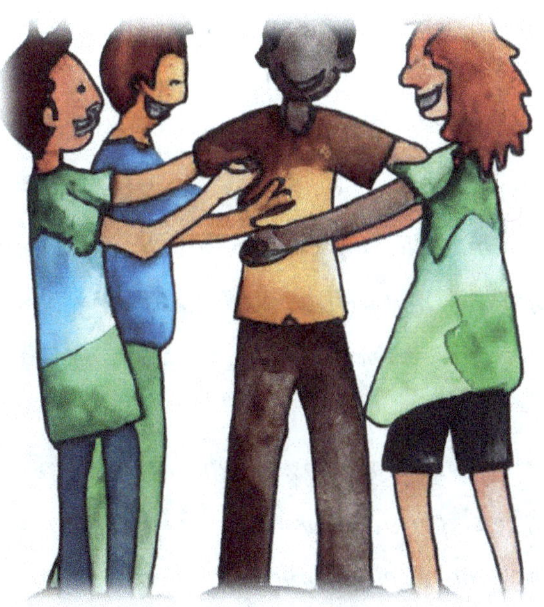

Kindness is a fundamental component of human nature and is required to develop a healthy and supportive community. Kindness is frequently characterized as being pleasant, giving, and caring, and it may manifest itself in various ways, ranging from little gestures of charity to more essential acts of selflessness. In this book, we examined many factors that contribute to misjudgments of people. However, one of the most significant factors that can overcome many consequences is being kind to others and how it may benefit both people and society.

Kindness to others has several advantages, both for the kind and the person being kind. Some of the advantages of being nice to others are as follows:

Increased happiness and well-being: Research has shown that showing kindness to others can increase happiness and well-being by reducing stress and anxiety and promoting feelings of joy and fulfillment.

Improved relationships: Kindness can help improve relationships by promoting trust, understanding, respect and strengthening social connections.

Increased resilience: Kindness can increase strength by fostering positive emotions and promoting a sense of belonging, which can help individuals to overcome adversity and cope with difficult situations.

Improved physical health: Research has shown that showing kindness to others can positively impact physical health by reducing the risk of heart disease, improving immune function, and reducing the effects of stress on the body.

There are many ways to show kindness to others, from simple acts of generosity to more significant acts of selflessness. Some of the ways that individuals can show kindness to others include:

Small acts of kindness: Small acts of kindness, such as smiling, holding the door open for someone, or offering a compliment, can have a significant impact on others and help create a positive and supportive environment.

Volunteering: Volunteering, such as helping out at a local food bank, visiting a senior center, or mentoring a young person, can help individuals to connect with others and make a positive impact on the community.

Supporting others: Supporting others, such as offering a listening ear or helping someone in need, can help to foster feelings of empathy, compassion, and understanding.

Practice random acts of kindness: Practicing random acts of kindness, such as paying for someone's meal or leaving a positive note for someone, can help to spread kindness and positivity in the community.

In summary, judging others can significantly negatively affect individuals and society, leading to shame, guilt, and self-doubt in those judged and contributing to division, hostility, and social unrest. To improve the adverse effects of judging others, it is crucial to adopt a more compassionate and understanding approach to others, cultivating empathy, challenging negative assumptions, and engaging in self-reflection. Doing so can promote a more positive and inclusive society and reduce the harmful effects of judging others.

Kindness to others is critical to establishing a healthy and supportive community. Kindness has several advantages, both for the person doing the act and for the person receiving it. It can assist in strengthening relationships, resilience, and physical and mental health. There are several ways to be nice to others, ranging from little acts of generosity to more significant acts of selflessness, and individuals can pick the techniques that work best for them. Individuals may help make the world more pleasant, helpful, and inclusive by being kind to others.

THE END